THE LITTLE
CURRY
COOKBOOK

THE LITTLE

CURRY

COOKBOOK

HERMES
HOUSE

This edition first published in the UK in 1998
by Hermes House

© 1998 Anness Publishing Limited

Hermes House is an imprint of
Anness Publishing Limited
Hermes House, 88-89 Blackfriars Road
London SE1 8HA

ISBN 1-901289-80-X

Publisher Joanna Lorenz
Senior Cookery Editor Linda Fraser
Assistant Editor Sarah Ainley
Copy Editor Jenni Fleetwood
Designers Patrick McLeavey & Jo Brewer
Illustrator Anna Koska
Photographers Karl Adamson, Edward Allwright,
David Armstrong, Steve Baxter, Amanda Heywood
& David Jorden
Recipes Rafi Fernandez, Shehzad Husain
& Manisha Kanani

For all recipes, quantities are given in both metric and
imperial measures, and, where appropriate, measures are
also given in standard cups and spoons. Follow one set,
but not a mixture, because they are not interchangeable.

Printed in China

1 3 5 7 9 10 8 6 4 2

Contents

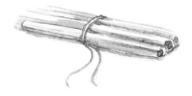

Introduction

Curries are hot favourites, not just for the tingle they bring to the tastebuds, but also for their incredible versatility and variety. The days when a curry eaten outside India meant some indeterminate meat in a thick, hot yellow sauce have long since gone. We now enjoy a wide range of these delicious dishes, and can readily discern differences between the hot spicy curries from the south of the Indian sub-continent and the creamy kormas and subtly spiced Kashmiri dishes of the north. We've discovered the delicately flavoured Thai and Malaysian curries, too, and ingredients like lemon grass, fresh coriander and root ginger are as familiar on our supermarket shelves as

peas and potatoes. Those same supermarkets also offer a remarkable range of curry mixes and pastes: some designed for long, slow cooking; others for the stir-fried quick curries that have become increasingly popular in an age where snacks need to be speedy but also flavoursome, colourful and nutritious. Balti cooking is becoming increasingly popular and its principal utensil, the twin-handled karahi, has joined the wok as one of the most useful items any modern kitchen can have.

Many cooks prefer to dry roast their own spices, then grind them, either with a mortar and pestle, or by using a coffee grinder kept specifically for the purpose. You can use a blender or food processor for some pastes, but this is not generally recommended. Not only does it put a strain on the blade and motor, but the spicy flavours are likely to linger, and curry-flavoured cakes are not to be recommended!

Store curry pastes in glass jars in the fridge. Ground spices benefit from being kept in a cool place, out of direct sunlight, and should be used as soon as possible. If you make or buy curry powder in bulk, store the surplus in the freezer. It will retain both colour and flavour.

The freezer is also a good place for fresh root ginger. Frozen ginger is very easy to grate or shave, and it thaws instantly when added to stir-fries, sauces or curries.

One of the reasons why curries have become so popular must be because of the sense of occasion they create. You can perch in front of the television with a plate of curry on your knee, but it is more practical, and infinitely more pleasurable, to make a real meal of it, setting the table with sambals, yogurt coolers and chutneys. Offer your guests poppadums while they savour the aromas originating from the kitchen, and make sure you have naan bread or parathas on hand for mopping up the delicious juices.

Curries offer wonderful opportunities for meatless meals. Countries where many of the inhabitants are vegetarians have naturally evolved a wide range of spicy and aromatic dishes based upon rice, pulses and vegetables. Most of these are as easy on the pocket as they are on the palate, and they make excellent family fare.

Cooking a curry need not be difficult or time-consuming. Recipes in this collection range from the simple and spicy Quick Curried Tuna to special occasion dishes like Saffron-scented Chicken Curry. Step-by-step instructions are easy to follow, and there are photographs of key stages as well as of every finished dish.

7

Spices & Aromatics

BAY LEAVES

Added whole or crumbled in spice mixes, bay leaves add an aromatic flavour to curries.

CARDAMOM

Pale green, beige or black cardamom pods yield pungent seeds. These are often used on their own, or whole pods may be added to curries for a more subtle flavour. Ground cardamom is a popular curry spice.

CHILLIES

Fresh green or red chillies are widely used. Handle them with care, as the juice will irritate sensitive skin, especially on the face. Wear gloves or wash your hands thoroughly after handling. Removing the seeds makes chillies less hot. Chillies are also available canned, dried or powdered.

CINNAMON

Sticks of cinnamon are used as flavouring, either whole or ground in spice mixes.

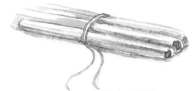

CLOVES

These nail-like flower buds are a popular curry spice. Use sparingly as they are quite pungent.

CORIANDER

A feathery member of the parsley family, coriander is used fresh, as a flavouring and garnish. The dried seeds (dhania) have a different taste, but are equally popular. Dried coriander seeds may be used whole, or they may be roasted or ground.

CUMIN

With a flavour reminiscent of caraway, cumin seeds are used whole or ground. The seeds are also known as jeera.

8

CURRY LEAVES

Aromatic curry leaves are used in much the same way as bay leaves. Use fresh if possible.

FENNEL SEEDS

Also known as barishap, these plump seeds have a mild aniseed flavour.

FENUGREEK

Both the leaves (methi) and seeds of fenugreek are used. It is also used ground as a spice mix.

GALANGAL

A member of the ginger family, also known as laos, this spice is often used in Thai cooking.

GINGER

Fresh root ginger looks plump, with a pinky-beige skin and creamy flesh. Store it in a well-ventilated vegetable rack or peel it and preserve it in sherry. Ginger can be frozen for grating.

MUSTARD SEEDS

Mustard seeds are dry roasted for extra flavour.

ONION SEEDS

The name is misleading: onion seeds are in fact black tear-shaped nigella seeds. Often used in vegetable dishes, they are also called kalonji.

SAFFRON

Staggeringly expensive to harvest, saffron threads are the dried stigmas of a type of crocus. They are valued for the flavour and colour they impart.

TAMARIND

The dried fruit of a tropical tree, tamarind has a sharp flavour. The dried seed pulp is diluted with water to make tamarind juice.

TURMERIC

Sometimes called "poor man's saffron" because it also tints food yellow, turmeric has a much less subtle taste. It is widely used in curry powders and pastes.

9

Techniques

SLICING CHILLIES

Handle chillies carefully; the juice will irritate delicate skin. Trim both ends and cut into neat rounds or, if the seeds are to be removed, cut in half lengthways, scrape out the seeds, then cut in strips, or dice.

CHOPPING FRESH GINGER

Break off a piece of ginger (about 2.5cm/1in), remove any rough ends, then peel. Slice cross-ways. Cut into slices, then dice. When grating ginger, it is not necessary to peel it.

CLARIFYING BUTTER

Simmer unsalted butter in a heavy-based pan until it separates, then carefully pour off the yellow liquid. Strain, cool and chill.

MAKING COCONUT MILK

Put 115g/4oz creamed coconut (in chunks) in a blender. Add 250ml/8fl oz/1 cup boiling water. Soak for 10 minutes, blend, then strain.

COOK'S TIP

Coconut milk is also available in a can or as a soluble powder. It can also be obtained directly from the coconut flesh – this will provide the creamiest milk.

10

Curry Mixes & Pastes

GARAM MASALA

Dry roast 10 dried red chillies, 3 short lengths of cinnamon stick and 2 curry leaves in a heavy-based frying pan for 2 minutes. Add 30ml/2 tbsp each of coriander and cumin seeds, and 5ml/1 tsp each of black peppercorns, cloves, fenugreek seeds and black mustard seeds. Dry roast for 8-10 minutes more, shaking the pan frequently. Cool and grind, then stir in 1.5ml/¼ tsp chilli powder.

RED CURRY PASTE

In a large mortar, mix 12 chopped red chillies, 4 chopped shallots, 2 crushed garlic cloves and 15ml/1 tbsp grated fresh root ginger. Add 2 chopped lemon grass stalks, 3 chopped kaffir lime leaves, 4 coriander roots, 10 black peppercorns, 5ml/1 tsp each coriander seeds and ground turmeric, 2.5ml/½ tsp each cumin seeds and shrimp paste, and a pinch of grated

cinnamon. Pound with a pestle until smooth. Stir in salt to taste and 30ml/2 tbsp vegetable oil. Scrape into a jar and store in the fridge.

TIKKA PASTE

Using a spice mill or mortar and pestle, grind 30ml/2 tbsp each of coriander and cumin seeds. Tip into a bowl and add 30ml/2 tbsp paprika; 15ml/1 tbsp each of garlic powder, garam masala, ground ginger and dried mint; 10ml/2 tsp chilli powder; 2.5ml/½ tsp ground turmeric and a generous pinch of salt. Mix well, then stir in 5ml/1 tsp lemon juice, 30ml/2 tbsp water and 150ml/¼ pint/⅔ cup white wine vinegar. Add a few drops of red and yellow food colouring. Heat 150ml/¼ pint/⅔ cup oil in a large heavy-based frying pan and fry the paste for 10 minutes or until the oil rises to the surface. Cool, then scrape into a sterilized jar. Store in the fridge.

11

Meat Dishes

Balti Lamb Tikka

INGREDIENTS

175ml/6fl oz/¾ cup natural yogurt
5ml/1 tsp ground cumin
5ml/1 tsp ground coriander
5ml/1 tsp chilli powder
5ml/1 tsp garam masala
1 garlic clove, crushed
5ml/1 tsp salt
30ml/2 tbsp chopped fresh coriander
30ml/2 tbsp lemon juice
450g/1lb lamb leg steak, cubed
30ml/2 tbsp corn oil
15ml/1 tbsp tomato purée
1 large green pepper, seeded and sliced
3 large fresh red chillies

SERVES 4

13

1 Mix the yogurt, dry spices, garlic, salt, coriander and lemon juice in a large bowl. Add to the lamb and stir to coat. Cover and leave for at least 1 hour to marinate.

2 Heat the oil in a deep round-bottomed frying pan or karahi. Lower the heat slightly and stir in the tomato purée. Using a slotted spoon, lift the lamb cubes out of the marinade, a few at a time, and add them to the pan. Cook, stirring frequently, for 7-10 minutes. As the cubes brown, push them to the edge of the pan so that more cubes can be added to the centre.

3 Add the green pepper slices and whole chillies to the lamb mixture. Serve as soon as the lamb is fully cooked and the peppers and chillies are hot.

Hot-and-Sour Meat & Lentil Curry

INGREDIENTS

4 garlic cloves
90ml/6 tbsp vegetable oil
5 fresh green chillies, chopped
2.5cm/1in piece of fresh root ginger, grated
2 bay leaves
5cm/2in piece of cinnamon stick
900g/2lb lean lamb, cubed
600ml/1 pint/2½ cups water
350g/12oz/1½ cups split red lentils, soaked
for 30 minutes in water to cover
2 potatoes, diced
1 aubergine, diced
50g/2oz/½ cup thawed frozen spinach,
drained
1 carrot, diced
4 onions, thinly sliced, deep-fried and drained
25g/1oz/1 cup chopped fresh fenugreek leaves
115g/4oz/4 cups chopped fresh coriander
50g/2oz/2 cups chopped fresh mint leaves
60ml/4 tbsp garam masala
5ml/1 tsp salt
10ml/2 tsp soft light brown sugar
60ml/4 tbsp tamarind juice
fresh coriander and mint sprigs, to garnish

SERVES 4-6

1 Crush 3 garlic cloves. Slice the fourth thinly and set it aside. Heat half the oil in a large saucepan and fry the green chillies, ginger and crushed garlic for 2 minutes. Add the bay leaves, cinnamon, lamb and water. Bring to the boil, then lower the heat and simmer for 15 minutes.

2 Drain the cooking liquid into a second pan and set the lamb aside. Drain the lentils and add them to the cooking liquid. Bring to the boil and cook for 20-30 minutes until very soft. Mash the lentils into the liquid.

3 Add the potatoes, aubergine, spinach and carrot to the lentils, with three-quarters of the onion slices. If the mixture is very thick, add a little water. Cook until the vegetables are tender, then mash them roughly.

4 Heat 15ml/1 tbsp of the remaining oil in a frying pan and cook all the leaves with the garam masala, salt and sugar for 2 minutes. Add the lamb and fry gently for 5 minutes, then add the contents of the frying pan to the lentil mixture. Stir well and cook over a low heat, stirring frequently, until the lamb is cooked through.

5 Stir in the tamarind juice. Fry the sliced garlic in the remaining oil until pale golden, pour it over the curry and top with the remaining fried onions and herb sprigs. Serve at once.

Spicy Minced Lamb Curry

INGREDIENTS

45ml / 3 tbsp vegetable oil
1 onion, finely chopped
5ml / 1 tsp ground cumin
5ml / 1 tsp ground coriander
5ml / 1 tsp chilli powder
2 garlic cloves, crushed
2.5cm / 1in piece of fresh root ginger, grated
2 fresh green chillies, finely chopped
675g / 1½lb lean minced lamb
300ml / ½ pint / 1¼ cups lamb stock or water
175g / 6oz / 1½ cups frozen peas
30ml / 2 tbsp lemon juice
salt
naan bread and natural yogurt, to serve

SERVES 4

2 Stir in the minced lamb. Fry, stirring frequently, for 5 minutes, then stir in the stock or water. Cover and simmer for 25 minutes, stirring occasionally.

3 Add the peas and lemon juice, with salt to taste. Cook for 10-15 minutes more, or until the lamb is tender and the peas are cooked. Serve with naan bread and natural yogurt.

1 Heat the oil in a large saucepan and fry the onion with the spices over a low heat for 5 minutes. Add the garlic, ginger and chillies and fry for 2-3 minutes more.

16

Beef Madras

INGREDIENTS

45ml/3 tbsp vegetable oil
1 large onion, finely chopped
4 cloves
4 green cardamom pods
2 fresh green chillies, finely chopped
2.5cm/1in piece of fresh root ginger,
finely chopped
2 garlic cloves, crushed
2 dried red chillies
15ml/1 tbsp curry paste
900g/2lb stewing beef, trimmed and cubed
10ml/2 tsp ground coriander
5ml/1 tsp ground cumin
2.5ml/½ tsp salt
150ml/¼ pint/⅔ cup beef stock
fresh coriander sprigs, to garnish

SERVES 4

1 Heat the oil in a large frying pan and fry the onion, cloves and cardamom pods over a medium heat for 5 minutes. Add the fresh green chillies, ginger and garlic. Crumble in the dried chillies. Fry, stirring, for 2 minutes.

2 Stir in the curry paste and fry for 2 minutes, then add the beef cubes, stirring to coat them in the spicy mixture. Fry for 5-6 minutes until lightly browned.

3 Add the ground coriander, cumin and salt. Pour in the stock and bring to the boil. Lower the heat, cover the pan and simmer for 1-1½ hours or until the meat is

tender. Garnish with fresh coriander sprigs. Serve with tomato rice, if you like.

Beef Vindaloo

INGREDIENTS

15ml/1 tbsp cumin seeds
seeds from 5 green cardamom pods
5ml/1 tsp fenugreek seeds
5ml/1 tsp black mustard seeds
4 dried red chillies, crumbled
5ml/1 tsp black peppercorns
2.5ml/½ tsp salt
2.5ml/½ tsp demerara sugar
60ml/4 tbsp white wine vinegar
60ml/4 tbsp vegetable oil
1 large onion, finely chopped
900g/2lb stewing beef, trimmed and cubed
2.5cm/1in piece of fresh root ginger,
finely chopped
1 garlic clove, crushed
10ml/2 tsp ground coriander
2.5ml/½ tsp ground turmeric
300ml/½ pint/1¼ cups water
plain and yellow rice, to serve

SERVES 4

1 Grind all the spice seeds with the chillies and peppercorns, using a mortar and pestle or spice mill. Scrape into a bowl and stir in the salt, sugar and vinegar; mix to a thin paste.

2 Heat 30ml/2 tbsp of the oil in a large frying pan and fry the onion for 10 minutes, then transfer it to a food processor, using a slotted spoon. Add the

spice mixture and process to a coarse paste. Scrape into a bowl and set aside.

3 Add the remaining oil to the pan. When hot, stir-fry the meat cubes for 10 minutes. As the cubes brown, remove them with a slotted spoon and set aside.

4 Add the ginger and garlic to the pan and fry for 2 minutes, then stir in the ground coriander and turmeric and fry for 2 minutes more. Add the onion and spice paste and fry for 5 minutes, stirring frequently, then return the meat to the pan.

5 Stir in the water and bring to the boil, then lower the heat, cover tightly and simmer the curry for 1-1½ hours, stirring occasionally, until the meat is tender. Serve with a mixture of boiled plain and yellow rice.

Stuffed Baby Aubergines & Peppers

INGREDIENTS

3 baby aubergines
2 even-size peppers
30ml/2 tbsp vegetable oil
1 onion, sliced
1 garlic clove, crushed
5ml/1 tsp grated fresh root ginger
5ml/1 tsp chilli powder
1.5ml/¼ tsp ground turmeric
5ml/1 tsp ground coriander
5ml/1 tsp salt
1 tomato, chopped
350g/12oz lean minced lamb
30ml/2 tbsp chopped fresh coriander
fresh coriander sprigs, to garnish
plain rice, to serve

SERVES 2-3

2 Heat half the oil in a saucepan and fry the onion until golden brown. Stir in the garlic and ginger, with the spices and salt. Stir-fry for 2 minutes, then add the tomato and minced lamb. Stir-fry for 7-10 minutes. Stir in the chopped fresh coriander.

3 Spoon the lamb mixture into the aubergine and pepper shells. Brush the exposed vegetables with the remaining oil. Bake for 30 minutes until cooked through and browned. Garnish, and serve with rice.

1 Preheat the oven to180°C/350°F/Gas 4. Slit the baby aubergines in half lengthways and scoop out and discard most of the flesh. Cut the tops off the peppers and remove the seeds. Place the aubergine and pepper shells in a lightly greased ovenproof dish.

20

Lamb & Apricot Curry

INGREDIENTS

900g / 2lb stewing lamb
30ml / 2 tbsp vegetable oil
2.5cm / 1in piece of cinnamon stick
4 green cardamom pods
1 onion, chopped
15ml / 1 tbsp curry paste
5ml / 1 tsp ground cumin
5ml / 1 tsp ground coriander
1.5ml / ¼ tsp salt
175g / 6oz / ¾ cup ready-to-eat dried apricots
350ml / 12fl oz / 1½ cups lamb stock
fresh coriander leaves, to garnish
yellow rice and mango chutney, to serve

SERVES 4

2 Stir in the curry paste and fry for 2 minutes. Sprinkle in the cumin, coriander and salt, stir well and cook for 2-3 minutes.

1 Trim any visible fat from the meat and cut into cubes. Heat the oil in a large heavy-based saucepan. Fry the cinnamon stick and cardamoms for 2 minutes, then

add the onion and fry over a low heat for 6-8 minutes until lightly browned.

3 Add the meat and apricots, stir well, then pour in the stock. Bring to the boil, lower the heat, cover the pan tightly and simmer for about an hour, or until the lamb is

tender. Garnish with fresh coriander leaves and serve with yellow rice and mango chutney.

Chicken Dishes

Balti Chilli Chicken

INGREDIENTS

75ml/5 tbsp corn oil
8 large fresh green chillies, slit
2.5ml/½ tsp mixed onion and cumin seeds
4 curry leaves
5ml/1 tsp grated fresh root ginger
5ml/1 tsp chilli powder
5ml/1 tsp ground coriander
5ml/1 tsp salt
2 onions, chopped
675g/1½lb skinless, boneless chicken
breasts, cubed
15ml/1 tbsp lemon juice
15ml/1 tbsp roughly chopped fresh mint
15ml/1 tbsp roughly chopped fresh coriander
10 cherry tomatoes

SERVES 4-6

23

1 Heat the oil in a deep round-bottomed frying pan or karahi. Fry the chillies over a medium heat until the skin starts to change colour, then add the onion and cumin seeds, curry leaves, ginger, chilli powder, ground coriander and salt. Stir-fry for 30 seconds, stirring constantly.

2 Add the onions and chicken to the frying pan. Stir-fry for 6-8 minutes, or until the chicken is cooked. Drizzle with the lemon juice and add the mint, coriander and cherry tomatoes. Heat through briefly and serve.

Chicken Tikka Masala

INGREDIENTS

675g / 1½lb skinless, boneless chicken breasts
60ml / 4 tbsp natural yogurt
90ml / 6 tbsp tikka paste
30ml / 2 tbsp vegetable oil
1 onion, chopped
1 garlic clove, crushed
1 fresh green chilli, seeded and chopped
2.5cm / 1in piece of fresh root ginger, grated
15ml / 1 tbsp tomato purée
15ml / 1 tbsp ground almonds
250ml / 8fl oz / 1 cup water
40g / 1½oz / 3 tbsp butter, melted
50ml / 3½ tbsp double cream
15ml / 1 tbsp lemon juice
fresh coriander sprigs and toasted cumin seeds, to garnish
natural yogurt and naan bread, to serve

SERVES 4

1 Cut the chicken into 2.5cm/1in cubes. Put the yogurt into a bowl and stir in three-quarters of the tikka paste. Add the chicken, stir to coat, cover and marinate for 20 minutes. Soak 8 wooden skewers in water for the same time.

2 Heat the oil in a saucepan and fry the onion, garlic, chilli and ginger for 5 minutes. Stir in the remaining tikka paste and fry for 2 minutes more, then lower

the heat and stir in the tomato purée, ground almonds and water. Bring to the boil, lower the heat and simmer the sauce for 15 minutes.

3 Meanwhile, preheat the grill. Drain the skewers and thread them with the chicken cubes. Brush the chicken with the melted butter and grill under a medium heat for 15 minutes, turning occasionally.

4 Transfer the tikka sauce to a food processor and process until smooth. Return to the clean pan and stir in the cream and the lemon juice. Remove the

chicken pieces from the skewers, add them to the sauce and simmer for 5 minutes. Garnish with fresh coriander sprigs and toasted cumin seeds and serve with natural yogurt and naan bread.

Red Chicken Curry

INGREDIENTS

600ml/1 pint/2½ cups coconut milk
15ml/1 tbsp red curry paste
450g/1lb skinless, boneless chicken
breasts, diced
30ml/2 tbsp fish sauce
15ml/1 tbsp granulated sugar
225g/8oz drained canned whole bamboo
shoots, rinsed and sliced
5 kaffir lime leaves, torn
salt and ground black pepper
2 fresh red chillies, chopped
fresh basil leaves and fresh mint leaves,
to garnish

SERVES 4-6

1 Pour half the coconut milk into a large heavy-based saucepan. Bring to the boil, stirring, until the milk separates, then add the red curry paste and cook for 2-3 minutes, stirring all the time.

2 Add the chicken, fish sauce and sugar to the pan and stir well. Cook for 3-5 minutes until the chicken changes colour, stirring constantly to prevent it from sticking to the pan.

3 Over a low heat, stir the remaining coconut milk, the bamboo shoots and kaffir lime leaves into the pan. Heat through gently. Add salt and pepper to  taste and check that the chicken is fully cooked. Transfer to a serving dish, garnish with the chopped red chillies and herbs. Serve at once.

Saffron-scented Chicken Curry

INGREDIENTS

4 skinless, boneless chicken breasts
garam masala
2 eggs, beaten
salt and ground black pepper
75g / 3oz / 6 tbsp ghee (clarified butter)
1 large onion, finely chopped
5cm / 2in piece of fresh root ginger, grated
4 garlic cloves, crushed
4 cloves
4 green cardamom pods
5cm / 2in piece of cinnamon stick
2 bay leaves
15-20 saffron threads
5ml / 1 tsp cornflour
150ml / ¼ pint / ⅔ cup natural yogurt
75ml / 5 tbsp double cream
50g / 2oz / ½ cup ground almonds

SERVES 4-6

1 Rub the chicken breasts with a little garam masala. Place the eggs in a shallow bowl and beat in a little salt and pepper. Heat the ghee in a large frying pan. Dip the chicken breasts in the egg, then fry them for 5 minutes on each side. Remove with tongs and keep hot.

2 Add the onion, ginger, garlic, cloves, cardamom pods, cinnamon and bay leaves to the ghee remaining in the pan. Fry for 5 minutes, until the onion is golden, then allow the mixture to cool slightly.

3 Stir the saffron and cornflour into the yogurt, add to the spice mixture and stir well. Return the chicken breasts to the pan, turning to coat them in the mixture. Cook over a low heat for about 20 minutes, or until the chicken is tender. Just before serving, fold in the cream and ground almonds and heat through briefly.

27

Curried Chicken with Tomatoes & Coriander

INGREDIENTS

30ml/2 tbsp corn oil
1.5ml/¼ tsp fenugreek seeds
1.5ml/¼ tsp onion seeds
2 onions, chopped
1 garlic clove, crushed
5ml/1 tsp grated fresh root ginger
400g/14oz can chopped tomatoes
5ml/1 tsp ground coriander
5ml/1 tsp chilli powder
5ml/1 tsp salt
30ml/2 tbsp lemon juice
3 skinless, boneless chicken breasts, quartered
30ml/2 tbsp chopped fresh coriander
3 fresh green chillies, chopped
½ red pepper, seeded and cut into chunks
½ green pepper, seeded and cut into chunks
fresh coriander sprigs, to garnish

SERVES 4

2 Put the tomatoes in a bowl. Add the ground coriander, chilli powder, salt and lemon juice. Mix well, then add the mixture to the saucepan. Raise the heat and stir-fry for 3 minutes.

3 Add the chicken pieces to the pan, turning to coat them in the spicy mixture. Stir-fry for 5-7 minutes, then sprinkle in the chopped fresh coriander with the chillies and peppers. Stir to mix.

4 Lower the heat, cover the pan and simmer the mixture for 10 minutes or until the chicken is cooked through and the sauce is thick and flavoursome. Garnish with fresh coriander sprigs and serve immediately.

1 Heat the oil in a saucepan and fry the fenugreek and onion seeds, shaking the pan frequently, until they begin to darken. Add the onions, garlic and ginger and fry for 5 minutes or until the onions are golden brown. Reduce the heat to the lowest setting while you prepare the spice mixture.

COOK'S TIP
Add a couple of bay leaves with the fenugreek and onion seeds, if you like. Remember to remove them before serving.

28

Chicken & Coconut Curry

INGREDIENTS

75g/3oz/1½ cups desiccated coconut
45ml/3 tbsp cold water
30ml/2 tbsp vegetable oil
4 black peppercorns
2.5ml/½ tsp cumin seeds
15ml/1 tbsp fennel seeds
15ml/1 tbsp coriander seeds
2 onions, finely chopped
2.5ml/½ tsp salt
8 small chicken pieces, such as thighs and
drumsticks, skinned
fresh coriander sprigs and lemon wedges,
to garnish

SERVES 4

2 Add the onions and fry for 5 minutes until lightly browned, then stir in the coconut and salt. Fry for 5 minutes, stirring frequently to prevent the mixture from sticking to the pan.

3 Tip the coconut mixture into a food processor or blender and process to a coarse paste. Spoon into a bowl and set aside until required.

4 Heat the remaining oil in the clean frying pan and fry the chicken pieces for 10 minutes. Add the coconut paste and cook over a low heat for 15-20 minutes, until the coconut mixture is golden and the chicken is fully cooked. Garnish with fresh coriander sprigs and lemon wedges and serve.

1 Mix the coconut and water in a bowl and leave to soak for 15 minutes. Meanwhile, heat 15ml/1 tbsp of the oil in a large frying pan. Add the peppercorns  and spice seeds and fry over a low heat for 3-4 minutes until the seeds start to splutter.

Chicken Dhansak

INGREDIENTS

*75g/3oz/scant ½ cup green lentils, soaked for
30 minutes in water to cover
475ml/16fl oz/2 cups vegetable stock
45ml/3 tbsp vegetable oil
5ml/1 tsp cumin seeds
2 curry leaves
1 onion, finely chopped
2.5cm/1in piece of fresh root ginger, chopped
1 fresh green chilli, finely chopped
5ml/1 tsp ground cumin
5ml/1 tsp ground coriander
1.5ml/¼ tsp chilli powder
1.5ml/¼ tsp salt
30ml/2 tbsp water
400g/14oz can chopped tomatoes
8 chicken thighs, skinned
60ml/4 tbsp chopped fresh coriander
5ml/1 tsp garam masala
fresh coriander sprigs, to garnish*

SERVES 4

1 Drain the lentils and put them in a large heavy-based saucepan. Add the stock and bring to the boil, then cover, lower the heat and simmer for 20 minutes. Set the pan aside.

2 Heat the oil in a large saucepan and fry the cumin seeds and curry leaves for 2 minutes. Add the onion, ginger and chilli and fry for 5 minutes. Stir in the ground spices, salt and water, then add the chopped tomatoes and the chicken. Cover and cook for 10-15 minutes.

3 Stir in the lentils, with any stock remaining in the pan. Add the chopped coriander and garam masala and cook for 10 minutes or until the chicken is tender. Garnish with fresh coriander sprigs and serve. Rice is the traditional accompaniment.

Chicken Biryani

INGREDIENTS

275g/10oz/1½ cups basmati rice, rinsed
2-3 cloves
1 cinnamon stick
10 cardamom pods
45ml/3 tbsp vegetable oil
3 onions, sliced
4 skinless, boneless chicken breasts, about
675g/1½lb, cubed
1.5ml/¼ tsp ground cloves
1.5ml/¼ tsp hot chilli powder
5ml/1 tsp ground cumin
5ml/1 tsp ground coriander
3 garlic cloves, crushed
5ml/1 tsp grated fresh root ginger
juice of 1 lemon
4 tomatoes, sliced
30ml/2 tbsp chopped fresh coriander
150ml/¼ pint/⅔ cup natural yogurt, plus
extra to serve
2.5ml/½ tsp saffron threads soaked in
10ml/2 tsp hot milk
150ml/¼ pint/⅔ cup water
toasted flaked almonds and fresh coriander
sprigs, to garnish

SERVES 4

1 Preheat the oven to 190°C/375°F/Gas 5. Bring a saucepan of lightly salted water to the boil and add the rice, cloves and cinnamon stick, with 5 of the cardamom pods. Boil for 2 minutes, then drain, leaving the spices in the rice.

2 Heat the oil in a frying pan and fry the onions for 8 minutes, until lightly browned. Add the chicken, with the ground spices. Remove the seeds from the remaining cardamom pods, bruise them lightly and add them to the pan with the garlic, ginger and lemon juice. Stir-fry for 5 minutes.

3 Tip the mixture into a casserole dish, lay the tomato slices on top and sprinkle with the fresh coriander. Spoon over the natural yogurt and top with the drained rice.

4 Drizzle the saffron liquid over the rice and pour over the water. Cover the casserole dish tightly and bake in the oven for 1 hour. Remove the whole spices. Serve at once, topped with the additional natural yogurt and garnished with the flaked almonds and fresh coriander sprigs.

Fish & Seafood

Parsi Prawn Curry

INGREDIENTS

3 onions
60ml/4 tbsp vegetable oil
6 garlic cloves, crushed
5ml/1 tsp chilli powder
7.5ml/1½ tsp ground turmeric
60ml/4 tbsp tamarind juice
5ml/1 tsp mint sauce
15ml/1 tbsp demerara sugar
salt
450g/1lb raw king prawns, peeled and deveined
75g/3oz/3 cups chopped fresh coriander

SERVES 4-6

1 Slice 1 onion finely; chop the remaining onions and set them aside. Heat the oil in a large frying pan and fry the sliced onion for 5-7 minutes, until golden  brown. In a small bowl, mix the garlic, chilli powder and turmeric with enough water to form a paste. Add this to the browned onion slices and simmer for 3 minutes.

2 Add the chopped onions to the pan and fry until translucent, stirring frequently. Stir in the tamarind juice, mint sauce, sugar and salt to taste. Simmer for 3 minutes more.

3 Pat the prawns dry with kitchen paper. Add them to the pan with just enough water to moisten. Stir-fry for 2-3 minutes, until the prawns turn a bright orange/pink colour.

4 Add the chopped fresh coriander and stir-fry over a high heat for 1 minute to thicken the sauce. Serve at once, garnished with a coriander sprig.

Indian Fish Curry

INGREDIENTS

30ml/2 tbsp vegetable oil
5ml/1 tsp cumin seeds
1 onion, chopped
1 red pepper, seeded and thinly sliced
1 garlic clove, crushed
2 fresh red chillies, finely chopped
2 bay leaves
2.5ml/½ tsp salt
5ml/1 tsp ground cumin
5ml/1 tsp ground coriander
5ml/1 tsp chilli powder
400g/14oz can chopped tomatoes
2 large potatoes, cut into 2.5cm/1in chunks
300ml/½ pint/1¼ cups fish stock
4 cod fillets
chapatis, to serve

SERVES 4

1 Heat the oil in a large deep-sided frying pan and fry the cumin seeds for 2 minutes until they start to splutter. Add the onion, red pepper, garlic, chillies and bay leaves. Fry for 5-7 minutes or until the onion is browned.

2 Stir in the salt, ground cumin, ground coriander and chilli powder. Cook for 3-4 minutes, stirring frequently.

3 Add the tomatoes and potatoes, stir lightly, then pour in the fish stock. Bring to the boil, then lower the heat and simmer for a further 10 minutes.

4 Place the fish fillets on top of the spiced vegetables, cover and simmer for 10 minutes or until the fish is cooked through. Serve with chapatis.

Thai Curried Prawns

INGREDIENTS

30ml/2 tbsp vegetable oil
30ml/2 tbsp Thai curry paste
450g/1lb raw king prawns, peeled and deveined
4 kaffir lime leaves, torn
1 lemon grass stalk, bruised and chopped
250ml/8fl oz/1 cup coconut milk
½ cucumber, seeded and cut into thin batons
30ml/2 tbsp fish sauce
10-15 fresh basil leaves
4 fresh green chillies, sliced, to garnish

SERVES 4-6

1 Heat the oil in a large frying pan. Add the curry paste and fry until bubbling and fragrant. Add the prawns, kaffir lime leaves and lemon grass. Stir-fry for 2-3 minutes, until the prawns turn a bright orange/pink colour.

2 Stir in the coconut milk. Bring to simmering point and cook over a gentle heat for 5 minutes, stirring occasionally, until the prawns are tender.

3 Stir in the cucumber, fish sauce and fresh basil leaves. Warm through briefly, garnish with the green chillies and serve at once.

COOK'S TIP

Fresh king prawns are really the best choice for this dish. Precooked or frozen king prawns can be used if fresh prawns are unavailable but are unlikely to give the same results.

White Fish Curry with Coconut

INGREDIENTS

juice of ½ lime
5ml / 1 tsp cider vinegar
salt
675g / 1½lb white fish fillet, skinned
225g / 8oz / 4 cups grated fresh coconut
2.5cm / 1in piece of fresh root ginger, grated
6 garlic cloves, roughly chopped
450g / 1lb tomatoes, chopped
45ml / 3 tbsp sunflower oil
350g / 12oz onions, roughly chopped
20 curry leaves
5ml / 1 tsp ground coriander
2.5ml / ½ tsp ground turmeric
5-10ml / 1-2 tsp chilli powder
300ml / ½ pint / 1¼ cups water
2.5ml / ½ tsp fenugreek seeds
2.5ml / ½ tsp cumin seeds
lime wedges, to garnish

SERVES 4

1 Mix the lime juice and vinegar in a large shallow bowl. Stir in a pinch of salt. Add the fish fillet, cover, and marinate for 30 minutes.

2 Put the grated coconut into a food processor or blender. Add the grated fresh root ginger, chopped garlic and tomatoes and process to a smooth paste.

3 Heat the oil in a large frying pan. Add the onions and cook for 5-7 minutes, until golden brown. Add the curry leaves, coriander, turmeric and chilli powder. Stir-fry for 1 minute.

4 Scrape the coconut paste into the pan. Mix well and cook for 3-4 minutes, stirring constantly. Pour in the water, bring to the boil, then lower the heat and simmer for 4 minutes.

5 Using a pestle, pound the fenugreek and cumin seeds together in a mortar. Lay the fish on top of the simmering sauce, sprinkle over the fenugreek mixture

and cook for 15 minutes, or until the fish is tender. Break the fish into chunks, garnish and serve.

Quick Curried Tuna

INGREDIENTS

45ml/3 tbsp vegetable oil
1.5ml/¼ tsp cumin seeds
2.5ml/½ tsp ground cumin
2.5ml/½ tsp ground coriander
2.5ml/½ tsp chilli powder
1.5ml/¼ tsp salt
2 garlic cloves, crushed
1 onion, thinly sliced
1 red pepper, seeded and thinly sliced
1 green pepper, seeded and thinly sliced
400g/14oz can tuna in oil or brine, drained
1 fresh green chilli, seeded and finely chopped
2.5cm/1in piece of fresh root ginger, grated
1.5ml/¼ tsp garam masala
5ml/1 tsp lemon juice
30ml/2 tbsp chopped fresh coriander
fresh coriander sprigs, to garnish
4 pitta breads and cucumber raita, to serve

SERVES 4

1 Heat the oil in a large frying pan. Fry the cumin seeds for 2 minutes, until they start to splutter. Stir in the ground cumin, ground coriander, chilli powder and salt. Cook for 2 minutes.

2 Add the garlic, onion and peppers to the frying pan and stir-fry for 5-6 minutes. Flake the tuna and add it to the pan, with the chilli and ginger. Cook for 5 minutes, turning the mixture gently with a spatula.

3 Sprinkle the garam masala over the tuna mixture, and add the lemon juice and fresh coriander. Cook for 3-4 minutes more. Preheat the grill.

4 Grill the pitta breads. Split the breads in half and pile the curry on top. Spoon a little cucumber raita over each portion and serve the rest separately, garnished with fresh coriander sprigs.

COOK'S TIP

To make cucumber raita, dice a 10cm/4in length of cucumber and stir into 300ml/ ½ pint/1¼ cups natural yogurt. Add 2.5ml/½ tsp each of salt and garam masala. Mix well and serve at room temperature.

Cod & Lentil Curry

INGREDIENTS

225g / 8oz / 1 cup red split lentils, soaked for
30 minutes in water to cover
1.5ml / ¼ tsp ground turmeric
600ml / 1 pint / 2½ cups fish stock
salt
30ml / 2 tbsp vegetable oil
7.5ml / 1½ tsp cumin seeds
15ml / 1 tbsp grated fresh root ginger
2.5ml / ½ tsp cayenne pepper
15ml / 1 tbsp lemon juice
60ml / 4 tbsp chopped fresh coriander
450g / 1lb cod fillets, skinned and cut
into large pieces
fresh coriander sprigs and lemon wedges,
to garnish

SERVES 4

1 Drain the lentils and put them in a saucepan with the turmeric and stock. Bring to the boil, lower the heat, cover and simmer for 20-25 minutes or until the lentils are just tender. Remove from the heat and add salt to taste.

2 Heat the oil in a small pan. Add the cumin seeds. When they splutter, add the ginger and cayenne. Stir-fry for a few seconds. Add to the lentils, with the lemon juice and half the coriander. Stir gently.

3 Lay the pieces of cod on top of the lentil mixture, cover the pan and cook over a low heat for 10-15 minutes, until the fish is cooked through.

4 Transfer the lentils and cod to warmed serving plates. Sprinkle over the remaining chopped coriander and garnish with the lemon wedges and fresh coriander sprigs. Serve at once.

42

Seafood Balti

INGREDIENTS

5ml/1 tsp each ground coriander, ground
cumin, chilli powder and salt
15ml/1 tbsp lemon juice
225g/8oz cod fillets, skinned and cubed
225g/8oz cooked prawns, peeled and deveined
6 crab sticks, halved lengthways
60ml/4 tbsp cornflour
150ml/¼ pint/⅔ cup corn oil
lime slices, to garnish
STIR-FRIED VEGETABLES
150ml/¼ pint/⅔ cup corn oil
2 onions, chopped
5ml/1 tsp onion seeds
½ cauliflower, separated into florets
115g/4oz French beans, cut into
2.5cm/1in lengths
175g/6oz can sweetcorn, drained
5ml/1 tsp each grated fresh root ginger, chilli
powder and salt
4 fresh green chillies, sliced
30ml/2 tbsp chopped fresh coriander

SERVES 4

1 Stir together the ground spices, salt and lemon juice. Add to the seafood in a bowl and mix with your hands. Sprinkle on the cornflour and mix again until well coated. Cover and chill for 1 hour.

2 Make the stir-fried vegetables. Heat the oil in a deep round-bottomed frying pan or karahi. Fry the onions and onion seeds for 5-7 minutes, until browned. Add all the remaining ingredients. Stir-fry for 7-10 minutes over a medium heat, making sure the cauliflower florets retain their shape.

3 Spoon the vegetables around the rim of a shallow dish. Keep hot. Heat the oil for the seafood in the clean pan. Fry the seafood pieces in batches for 2-3 minutes, until golden brown. Remove with a slotted spoon, drain on kitchen paper and spoon into the centre of the stir-fried vegetables. Serve at once, garnished with lime slices.

Vegetable Dishes

Mixed Vegetable Curry

INGREDIENTS

675g / 1½lb / 4 cups mixed vegetables
(potatoes, carrots, beans, peas, cauliflower,
cabbage, mange-touts and mushrooms)
45ml / 3 tbsp vegetable oil
10ml / 2 tsp roasted cumin seeds
or ground cumin
5ml / 1 tsp mustard seeds
5ml / 1 tsp onion seeds
5ml / 1 tsp ground turmeric
6-8 curry leaves
3 garlic cloves, crushed
2 dried red chillies
5ml / 1 tsp granulated sugar
2.5ml / ½ tsp salt
300ml / ½ pint / 1¼ cups natural yogurt,
mixed with 10ml / 2 tsp cornflour
salt and ground black pepper

SERVES 4-6

1 Prepare the vegetables according to type, cutting them into pieces of about the same size. Bring a large saucepan of water to the boil, add the potatoes and carrots and cook for about 15 minutes until almost tender. Add the remaining vegetables and cook until crisp-tender. Drain well.

2 Heat the oil in a wok or large frying pan and fry the spices with the garlic and whole dried chillies until the garlic is golden and the chillies are almost burnt. Reduce the heat.

3 Fold in the drained vegetables, sprinkle the sugar and salt over them and toss to mix. Gradually add the yogurt mixture, stirring over a low heat until the sauce  thickens and the vegetables are hot. Season with salt and pepper and serve at once.

Corn Cob Curry

INGREDIENTS

4 whole fresh corn cobs
90ml/6 tbsp vegetable oil
1 large onion, finely chopped
2 garlic cloves, crushed
5cm/2in piece of fresh root ginger, grated
2.5ml/1/2 tsp ground turmeric
2.5ml/1/2 tsp onion seeds
2.5ml/1/2 tsp cumin seeds
2.5ml/1/2 tsp five-spice powder
1.5ml/1/4 tsp chilli powder
6-8 curry leaves
2.5ml/1/2 tsp granulated sugar
250ml/8fl oz/1 cup natural yogurt
lime or lemon slices, to garnish

SERVES 4-6

I Cut the corn cobs in half, using a large, sharp knife. Heat the oil in a large frying pan and fry the half cobs until golden brown on all sides. Transfer  the corn to a plate. Pour off all but 30ml/2 tbsp oil from the pan and set the pan aside.

2 Mix the onion, garlic and ginger in a mortar and grind with a pestle. Alternatively, use a spice mill. Stir in the spices, curry leaves and sugar.

3 Reheat the oil and fry the onion mixture over a gentle heat until the spices have blended well and the oil has separated from the paste. Cool slightly, then gradually stir in the yogurt. Mix to a smooth, golden sauce.

4 Return the pieces of corn to the pan and turn to coat in the sauce. Reheat gently for 10 minutes, garnish with lime or lemon slices and serve.

46

Cumin-spiced Marrow Curry

INGREDIENTS

1 marrow, about 900g/2lb
60ml/4 tbsp vegetable oil
15ml/1 tbsp cumin seeds
2 fresh red chillies, seeded and finely chopped
60ml/4 tbsp water
115g/4oz tender young spinach leaves
175ml/6fl oz/¾ cup single cream
salt and ground black pepper
plain or spiced rice, to serve

SERVES 4

1 Peel the marrow and cut it in half. Remove the seeds and cube the flesh. Heat the oil in a frying pan. Add the cumin seeds and chillies. Cook for 1 minute.

2 Add the marrow and water to the pan. Cover tightly and simmer for 8 minutes, until the marrow is just tender. Remove the lid and cook for 2 minutes more.

3 Add the spinach leaves, replace the lid and cook gently for 1 minute. Stir in the cream and slightly raise the heat. Cook for 2 minutes, then season with salt and pepper to taste and serve at once with plain or spiced rice.

47

Vegetable Kashmiri

INGREDIENTS

10ml/2 tsp cumin seeds
8 black peppercorns
seeds from 2 green cardamom pods
5cm/2in piece of cinnamon stick, crumbled
2.5ml/½ tsp grated nutmeg
45ml/3 tbsp oil
1 fresh green chilli, chopped
2.5cm/1in piece of fresh root ginger, grated
2.5ml/½ tsp chilli powder
2.5ml/½ tsp salt
2 large potatoes, cut into 2.5cm/1in cubes
225g/8oz cauliflower
225g/8oz okra
150ml/¼ pint/⅔ cup natural yogurt,
mixed with 5ml/1 tsp cornflour
150ml/¼ pint/⅔ cup vegetable stock
toasted flaked almonds and fresh coriander
sprigs, to garnish

SERVES 4

1 Use a mortar and pestle or a spice mill to grind the cumin seeds, black peppercorns, cardamom pods, cinnamon stick and nutmeg to a fine powder.

2 Heat the oil in a large saucepan and fry the chilli and ginger for 2 minutes over a medium heat, stirring all the time. Add the chilli powder, salt and ground spice mixture and fry for 2-3 minutes, continuing to stir to stop the spices from sticking.

3 Add the potato cubes, stir to coat them in the spice mixture, then cover the pan and cook for 10 minutes over a low heat, stirring occasionally.

4 Meanwhile, break the cauliflower into florets. Slice the okra thickly. Add both to the pan, stir lightly and cook for 5 minutes.

5 Pour in the yogurt mixture and the stock. Bring to just below the boil, then lower the heat and simmer for 20 minutes. Transfer to a bowl and serve at once, garnished with toasted almonds and fresh coriander sprigs.

COOK'S TIP

Take care not to touch your face when preparing chillies. Use gloves if possible, or wash your hands thoroughly immediately after slicing the chillies, as their oil can burn sensitive skin.

Curried Stuffed Peppers

INGREDIENTS

15ml/1 tbsp sesame seeds
15ml/1 tbsp white poppy seeds
5ml/1 tsp coriander seeds
60ml/4 tbsp desiccated coconut
½ onion, sliced
2.5cm/1in piece of fresh root ginger, peeled and thinly sliced
4 garlic cloves, sliced
handful of fresh coriander, chopped
6 fresh green chillies
60ml/4 tbsp vegetable oil
2 potatoes, boiled and roughly mashed
salt
6 even-size peppers of assorted colours
30ml/2 tbsp sesame oil
5ml/1 tsp cumin seeds
60ml/4 tbsp tamarind juice

SERVES 4-6

1 Dry-fry the sesame, poppy and coriander seeds in a large frying pan, then add the coconut and roast, stirring, until golden. Add the onion, ginger, garlic and fresh coriander with 2 whole chillies; roast for 5 minutes more. Cool, then tip into a mortar and grind to a paste with a pestle.

2 Heat 30ml/2 tbsp of the vegetable oil in a frying pan. Fry the spice paste gently for 5 minutes. Stir in the mashed potato, with salt to taste. Mix well.

3 Trim the base of each pepper so that it will stand upright, then slice off the lids and reserve. Remove the seeds and pith, keeping the peppers intact, then fill them with the spiced potato mixture. Replace the lids.

4 Slit the remaining chillies. Heat the sesame oil and remaining vegetable oil in a large frying pan. Add the chillies and cumin seeds and fry until the chillies turn white. Add the tamarind juice and bring to the boil. Stand the peppers in the pan, cover and cook until tender. Serve hot or cool, or chill for several days to let the spices mature before serving cold.

Cauliflower & Potato Curry

INGREDIENTS

450g/1lb potatoes, cut into 2.5cm/1in cubes
30ml/2 tbsp vegetable oil
5ml/1 tsp cumin seeds
1 fresh green chilli, finely chopped
1 large cauliflower, about 450g/1lb, broken into florets
1.5ml/¼ tsp chilli powder
5ml/1 tsp ground coriander
5ml/1 tsp ground cumin
2.5ml/½ tsp ground turmeric
2.5ml/½ tsp salt
chopped fresh coriander, to garnish

SERVES 4

1 Bring a large saucepan of lightly salted water to the boil. Add the potatoes and parboil for 10 minutes. Drain well and set aside.

2 Heat the oil in a large heavy-based frying pan or wok. Fry the cumin seeds for 2 minutes, stirring frequently, until they start to splutter. Add the chopped chilli to the pan. Continue to fry the mixture for 1 minute more.

3 Add the cauliflower florets, turning them gently to coat them in the seed and chilli mixture. Stir-fry for 5 minutes.

4 Add the potatoes, the chilli powder, ground spices and salt. Stir-fry for 7-10 minutes over a medium heat or until the potatoes are tender, making sure the cauliflower florets retain their shape. Garnish with fresh coriander and serve.

Mushroom & Okra Curry

INGREDIENTS

2 garlic cloves, roughly chopped
2.5cm / 1in piece of fresh root ginger, grated
1-2 fresh red chillies, chopped
175ml / 6fl oz / ¾ cup cold water
15ml / 1 tbsp sunflower oil
5ml / 1 tsp coriander seeds
5ml / 1 tsp cumin seeds
5ml / 1 tsp ground cumin
seeds from 2 green cardamom pods, ground
pinch of ground turmeric
400g / 14oz can chopped tomatoes
450g / 1lb mushrooms, quartered if large
225g / 8oz okra, trimmed and sliced
30ml / 2 tbsp chopped fresh coriander
basmati rice, to serve
MANGO RELISH
2 ripe mangoes
1 small garlic clove, crushed
1 onion, finely chopped
10ml / 2 tsp grated fresh root ginger
1 fresh red chilli, finely chopped
pinch each of salt and sugar

SERVES 4

1 Make the fresh mango relish. Peel the mangoes. Cut the flesh off the stone and place it in a bowl. Using a fork, mash the flesh to a purée, then stir in the garlic, onion, ginger, chilli, salt and sugar. Cover and set aside.

2 Make the curry. Put the garlic, ginger and chillies in a blender or food processor. Add 45ml/3 tbsp of the water and purée them until smooth.

3 Heat the oil in a large shallow pan. Add the whole coriander and cumin seeds and cook for a few seconds until they start to splutter. Add the ground cumin, ground cardamom seeds and turmeric; stir-fry for 1 minute more.

4 Tip in the garlic paste from the blender, then add the tomatoes, remaining water, mushrooms and okra. Stir to mix. Bring to the boil, lower the heat, cover and simmer for 5 minutes.

5 Remove the lid, raise the heat slightly and cook for 5-10 minutes more, until the okra is tender. Stir in the fresh coriander and serve with basmati rice and the mango relish.

Rice & Pulses

Spinach Dhal

INGREDIENTS

175g/6oz/1 cup chana dhal or yellow
split peas
175ml/6fl oz/¾ cup water
30ml/2 tbsp oil
1.5ml/¼ tsp black mustard seeds
1 onion, thinly sliced
2 garlic cloves, crushed
2.5cm/1in piece of fresh root ginger, grated
1 fresh red chilli, finely chopped
275g/10oz frozen spinach, thawed
1.5ml/¼ tsp chilli powder
2.5ml/½ tsp ground coriander
2.5ml/½ tsp garam masala
2.5ml/½ tsp salt

SERVES 4

1 Wash the chana dhal or split peas in several changes of cold water. Drain, put into a bowl and cover with fresh cold water. Leave to soak for 30 minutes.

2 Drain the pulses again and put them in a large saucepan with the measured water. Bring to the boil, lower the heat, cover and simmer for 20-25 minutes until soft. Drain and put to one side.

3 Meanwhile, heat the oil in a large frying pan. Fry the mustard seeds for 2 minutes, stirring until they start to splutter, then add the onion, garlic, ginger and chilli.  Stir-fry for 5-6 minutes. Add the spinach. Cook for 10 minutes or until the spinach is dry and the liquid has been absorbed. Stir in the remaining spices and salt and cook for 2-3 minutes.

4 Add the pulses to the spinach mixture. Cook for about 5 minutes, stirring frequently. Serve at once.

Curried Chick-Peas

INGREDIENTS

30ml/2 tbsp vegetable oil
30ml/2 tbsp ground coriander
30ml/2 tbsp ground cumin
2.5ml/^{1}/2 tsp turmeric
2.5ml/^{1}/2 tsp salt
2.5ml/^{1}/2 tsp sugar
30ml/2 tbsp flour paste
450g/1 lb boiled chick-peas, drained
2 fresh green chillies, chopped
1 piece of fresh root ginger, grated
75g/3 oz/3 cups chopped fresh coriander
2 tomatoes, chopped
POTATO CAKES
450g/1 lb potatoes, boiled and roughly mashed
4 fresh green chillies, chopped
50g/2 oz/2 cups chopped fresh coriander
25ml/1^1/2 tbsp ground cumin
15ml/1 tbsp dry mango powder
salt

SERVES 10-12

1 Make the curried chick-peas. Heat the oil in a saucepan and fry the coriander, cumin, turmeric, salt, sugar and flour paste until the water has evaporated and the oil separated.

2 Add the chick-peas, chillies, fresh ginger, coriander and the tomatoes. Toss well and simmer gently for 5 minutes. Transfer to a serving dish and keep warm.

3 Make the potato cakes. In a large bowl, mix together the mashed potato, the green chillies, coriander, cumin, dry mango powder and salt. Blend well.

4 Shape the potato mixture into little cakes, using your hands. Heat the oil and fry the cakes until golden brown. Transfer to a warmed dish and serve at once with the chick-peas.

Curried Mung Beans & Potatoes

INGREDIENTS

2 potatoes, cut into chunks
175g/6oz/1 cup mung beans, rinsed
750ml/1¼ pints/3 cups water
30ml/2 tbsp vegetable oil
2.5ml/½ tsp cumin seeds
1 green chilli, finely chopped
1 garlic clove, crushed
2.5cm/1in piece of fresh root ginger, grated
1.5ml/¼ tsp ground turmeric
2.5ml/½ tsp chilli powder
5ml/1 tsp salt
5ml/1 tsp sugar
4 curry leaves
5 tomatoes, peeled and finely chopped
15ml/1 tbsp tomato purée
curry leaves, to garnish

SERVES 4

1 Bring a saucepan of lightly salted water to the boil. Add the potatoes and parboil for 10 minutes, then drain. Place the mung beans in a second saucepan, and pour over the measured water. Bring to the boil, lower the heat, cover and simmer for about 30 minutes.

2 Meanwhile, heat the oil in a saucepan and fry the cumin seeds until they start to splutter. Add the chilli, garlic and ginger and fry for 3-4 minutes. Stir in the turmeric, chilli powder, salt and sugar and cook for 2 minutes, stirring to prevent the mixture from sticking.

3 Add the curry leaves, tomatoes and tomato purée to the spice mixture. Simmer, stirring occasionally, for 5 minutes until the sauce thickens. When the mung beans are soft and have absorbed most of the liquid, add the spicy sauce. Add the potatoes to the pan and mix lightly. Serve at once, garnished with curry leaves.

Madras Sambal

INGREDIENTS

*225g/8oz/1 cup red split lentils, soaked for
30 minutes in water to cover
2.5ml/½ tsp ground turmeric
600ml/1 pint/2½ cups water
2 large potatoes, cut into 2.5cm/1in chunks
30ml/2 tbsp vegetable oil
2.5ml/½ tsp black mustard seeds
1.5ml/¼ tsp fenugreek seeds
4 curry leaves
1 onion, thinly sliced
115g/4oz French beans, cut into
2.5cm/1in lengths
5ml/1 tsp salt
2.5ml/½ tsp chilli powder
15ml/1 tbsp lemon juice
60ml/4 tbsp desiccated coconut
toasted dessicated coconut, to garnish*

SERVES 4

2 Meanwhile, parboil the potato cubes in a saucepan of boiling water for 10 minutes. Drain well and set aside.

3 Heat the oil in a large frying pan and fry the mustard and fenugreek seeds with the curry leaves for 2-3 minutes until the seeds start to splutter. Add the onion and French beans and stir-fry for 7-8 minutes. Finally, add the potatoes and cook for 2 minutes more.

4 Stir in the lentils with the salt, chilli powder and lemon juice. Simmer for 2 minutes. Stir in the desiccated coconut and simmer for 5 minutes more. Garnish with toasted coconut and serve.

1 Drain the lentils and put them in a heavy-based saucepan. Add the turmeric and the measured water. Bring to the boil, then lower the heat, cover and simmer for 20-25 minutes or until the lentils are soft and have absorbed most of the liquid.

Vegetable Pilau

INGREDIENTS

225g/8oz/generous 1 cup basmati rice
30ml/2 tbsp oil
2.5ml/½ tsp cumin seeds
2 bay leaves
4 green cardamom pods
4 cloves
1 onion, finely chopped
1 carrot, finely diced
50g/2oz/½ cup frozen peas, thawed
50g/2oz/½ cup frozen sweetcorn, thawed
25g/1oz/¼ cup cashew nuts, lightly fried
1.5ml/¼ tsp ground cumin
475ml/16fl oz/2 cups water

SERVES 4-6

60

1 Put the basmati rice into a bowl, add cold water to cover and leave to soak for 30 minutes. Meanwhile, heat the oil in a large frying pan and fry the cumin  seeds for 2 minutes. Add the bay leaves, cardamom pods and cloves and fry for 2 minutes.

2 Add the onion and stir-fry for 5-7 minutes, until lightly browned, then add the carrot and stir-fry for 3-4 minutes.

3 Drain the rice and add it to the frying pan with the peas, sweetcorn and cashew nuts. Stir-fry for 4-5 minutes.

4 Add the cumin and pour over the measured water. Bring to the bowl, lower the heat, cover and simmer for 15 minutes, until all the water has been absorbed. Remove from the heat, but leave the lid on for the next 10 minutes. Just before serving, fork over the rice.

Egg & Lentil Curry

INGREDIENTS

75g/3oz/scant ½ cup green lentils, soaked for 30 minutes in water to cover
750ml/1¼ pints/3 cups vegetable stock
6 eggs
30ml/2 tbsp vegetable oil
3 cloves
1.5ml/¼ tsp black peppercorns
1 onion, finely chopped
2 fresh green chillies, finely chopped
2 garlic cloves, crushed
2.5cm/1in piece of fresh root ginger, peeled and finely chopped
30ml/2 tbsp curry paste
400g/14oz can chopped tomatoes
2.5ml/½ tsp sugar
175ml/6fl oz/¾ cup water
2.5ml/½ tsp garam masala

SERVES 4

1 Drain the lentils and put them in a large heavy-based saucepan. Add the stock. Bring to the boil, then lower the heat, cover and simmer for 20 minutes or until the lentils are soft. Drain and set aside.

2 Cook the eggs in a saucepan of boiling water for 10 minutes. Cool under cold running water, then peel and cut in half lengthways.

3 Heat the oil in a large saucepan. Fry the cloves and peppercorns for 2 minutes, then add the onion, chillies, garlic and ginger. Stir-fry the mixture for 5-6 minutes.

4 Stir in the curry paste. Fry for 2 minutes, then add the tomatoes, sugar and water. Mix well. Simmer for 5 minutes to thicken the sauce. Stir in the lentils and garam masala, then add the eggs. Spoon the sauce over them but do not break them up. Cover and simmer for 10 minutes, then serve.

Mixed Bean Curry

INGREDIENTS

50g / 2 oz / 1/3 cup red kidney beans
50g / 2 oz / 1/3 cup black-eyed beans
50g / 2 oz / 1/3 cup haricot beans
50g / 2 oz / 1/3 cup flageolet beans
30ml / 2 tbsp vegetable oil
5ml / 1 tsp cumin seeds
1 onion, finely chopped
2 garlic cloves, crushed
2.5cm / 1 in piece fresh root ginger, grated
2 green chillies, finely chopped
30ml / 2 tbsp curry paste
2.5ml / 1/2 tsp salt
400g / 14 oz can chopped tomatoes
30ml / 2 tbsp tomato purée
250ml / 8 fl oz / 1 cup water
30ml / 2 tbsp chopped fresh coriander, plus extra to garnish

SERVES 4

1 Put all the beans into a large bowl and cover with cold water. Leave them to soak overnight, mixing occasionally, to ensure they are evenly soaked.

2 Drain the beans and put them into a large heavy-based saucepan with double the volume of cold water. Boil vigorously for 10 minutes. Skim off any scum. Cover the pan and simmer for 1 1/2 hours or until the beans have softened.

3 Heat the oil in a large saucepan and fry the cumin seeds and mustard seeds for 2 minutes until the seeds begin to splutter. Add the onion, garlic, ginger and chilli and fry for 5 minutes.

4 Add the curry paste and fry for 2-3 minutes more, stirring, then add the salt. Add the tomatoes, tomato purée and water and simmer for 5 minutes.

5 Add the drained beans and the fresh coriander. Cover and simmer for about 30-40 minutes until the sauce thickens and the beans are cooked. Garnish with chopped fresh coriander.

Index